Home for
HENRYs

Home for
HENRYs

Meet the New Customers
Home Décor Marketers
Are Searching For:

High-Earners-Not-Rich-Yet

Pamela N. Danziger

PMP

Paramount Market Publishing, Inc.

Paramount Market Publishing, Inc.
274 North Goodman Street, STE D-214
Rochester, NY 14607
www.paramountbooks.com
607-275-8100

Publisher: James Madden
Editorial Director: Doris Walsh

This publication is designed to provide accurate and
authoritative information in regard to the subject matter
covered. It is sold with the understanding that the publisher is
not engaged in rendering legal, accounting, or other professional
services. If legal advice or other expert assistance is required,
the services of a competent professional should be sought.

All trademarks are the property of their respective companies.

Cataloging in Publication Data available
ISBN-10: 1-941688-46-2 | ISBN-13: 978-1-941688-46-5 *paper*
eISBN-13: 978-1-941688-46-5

Dedication

For my home-loving partner, Greg

Contents

Making a Home For HENRYs

During the depths of the Great Recession, when just about every other home furnishings marketer was struggling to stay afloat, **Restoration Hardware** unexpectedly discovered its path to growth and success. While its lower priced lines remained on the shelves and on the sales floor, the company's premium, higher-priced offerings counterintuitively kept selling. At first the company couldn't figure out why.

Digging deeper, Restoration Hardware found the customers keeping the high-end of its business alive were the young affluent HENRYs – high-earners-not-rich-yet. With that discovery, the company charted a course to grow offering more luxury products and experiences that those new customers craved. Not luxury as traditional home furnishing marketers think of luxury, but luxury in a brand new style tailored to the lifestyle and budget of HENRYs.

Today Restoration Hardware has reinvented itself. Now christened RH, it has focused on new customers with new lines in grand new gallery shopping experiences that have captured the imaginations and home furnishings dollars of HENRYs. This strategic shift has produced exponential growth, including 24 consecutive quarters of double-digit sales gains, with revenue up 54 percent from 2010–2012, followed by a 13 percent increase in 2013, 20 percent increase in 2014 and 13 percent in 2015. This explosive growth propelled company sales from $958 million in 2012 to $2.1 billion in 2015.

Help for Home Marketers in Search of New Customers

In survey after survey among business executives conducted by Unity Marketing, finding new customers rises to the top as their most pressing need and biggest challenge. Take for example, a recent survey among home furnishings marketers aimed at the high-end. Over half rated finding new customers their top challenge.

This book is a guide for home furnishings marketers to discover their best new customer prospects: the HENRYs that today number roughly 27 million households. These are customers with high levels of income ($100,000 to $249,900) and the need and desire for home furnishings.

**Affluent Household Spending on
Home Luxury Goods**

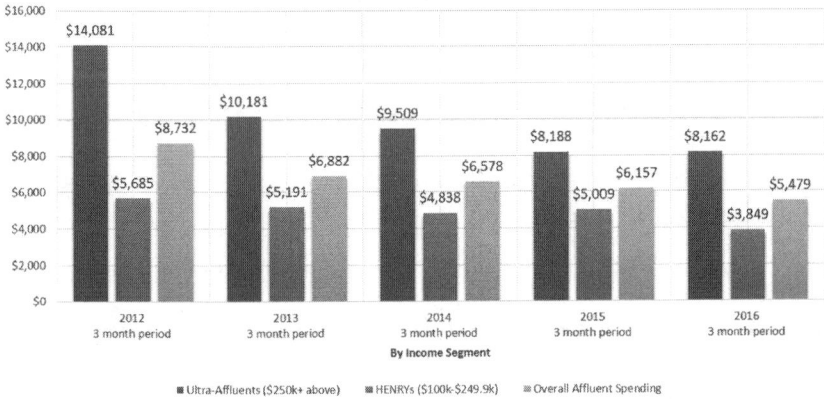

	2012 3 month period	2013 3 month period	2014 3 month period	2015 3 month period	2016 3 month period
Ultra-Affluents ($250k+ above)	$14,081	$10,181	$9,509	$8,188	$8,162
HENRYs ($100k-$249.9k)	$5,685	$5,191	$4,838	$5,009	$3,849
Overall Affluent Spending	$8,732	$6,882	$6,578	$6,157	$5,479

By Income Segment

What's more the HENRY consumer segment is rapidly growing, as Millennials and GenXers mature in their careers and grow their incomes to become part of the nation's top 20 percent. Each year since 2010 over a million households have been added to the HENRYs' ranks. Since 2010, the number of HENRY households have increased by 23.1 percent, five times faster than the national average, which increased only 3.9 percent in the same time.

Growth in Number of American Households
2010-2015

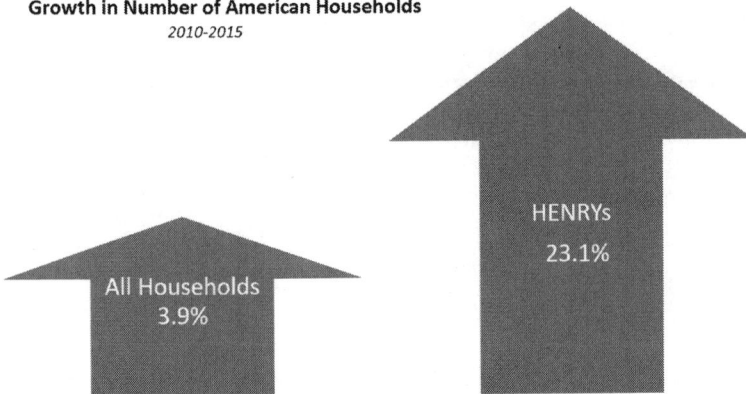

HENRYs
23.1%

All Households
3.9%

Meet the home-hungry HENRYs – your now and future best customer prospects.

West Elm Knows What HENRYs Want

Williams-Sonoma Inc. just released its 2015 annual report with news that its 2015 net revenues rose 5.9 percent over 2014, with both its e-commerce (6.4 percent) and retail (5.4 percent) operations posting increases. But not all of the Williams-Sonoma brands could boast such dramatic growth. The luxury-leaning Williams-Sonoma flagship brand was up a measly 1.1 percent, while mass-market targeted **Pottery Barn** eked out 1.9 percent growth. **West Elm,** its hip, urban contemporary brand, led with a 14.8 percent gain, reaching $821 million in sales.

What made West Elm the growth engine for the company, while other Williams-Sonoma brands languished? West Elm knows what young HENRY customers want in home furnishings and shopping experiences and delivers it to them. Williams-Sonoma? Not so much.

HENRYs are the key demographic customer for the future home market

HENRYs are the key demographic customer for the future home market. Young HENRYs, aged 24–34 years, have already reached affluent levels of income ($100k-$249.9k), but not yet hit their peak earning years. That will happen around the middle of the next decade.

It is unlikely that once young HENRYs reach Ultra-affluent income levels of $250k+, putting them squarely in the target market for luxury brands like Williams-Sonoma, that they will transfer loyalty. West Elm is perfectly positioned to keep their core customers coming back, even as they age and their incomes rise.

West Elm is a connected brand for a connecting generation

Now with 87 locations, less than half the number of stores as Pottery Barn and Williams-Sonoma, West Elm's secret sauce is its commitment to connect with customers by creating meaningful experiences in and through its stores. While it is now an international retailer, with stores in Australia, U.K. and Mexico, each store strives to be a vital part of its local community. West Elm stores are customized to the local market. Its 'think small, think local, think young' strategy is key to its success.

West Elm with its modern design sensibility is perfectly in tune with not just the home decorating preferences of young HENRYs, but their values, attitudes and lifestyles. Examples:

- **Handcrafted, Fair Trade goods:** It has committed with the Clinton Global Initiative to source $35 million worth of handmade goods over the next two years. The result: More than 20 percent of the company's products will be handmade.

- **Made in USA:** West Elm customers wear Carhartt jackets and carry Filson bags and want American heritage brands, so the company will source more made in USA product.

- **Supporting craftspeople:** In a unique partnership with internet-crafts site **Etsy,** West Elm showcases selective Etsy sellers in its catalogs and in popup shops at various stores. Early success of this venture has resulted in West Elm becoming a partner in a new Etsy Wholesale venture which connects Etsy craft sellers with brick-and-mortar shops, including independent retailers and museum shops.

- **More kitchen and home goods:** West Elm has spun off 'West Elm Market' to showcase kitchen and other home goods, 75 percent of which are made in the U.S. The West Elm Market stores, some of which are stand-alone and others are stores-within-a-store, also feature a coffee bar.

- **Home decorating services:** West Elm offers free decorator services where the decorator visits the customer's home to help clients pick out products and create a decorating statement in their home.

- **Classes and special events:** Classes, like basics of fermentation and container gardening, are taught by store staffers or local entrepreneurs through partnership with Skillshare and other organizations. Classes are not focused so much on selling store product, but helping their customers enhance their lifestyles. To make West Elm a more vital part of the community and caring partner of the customers is the goal of these classes. That class attendees return to the store more often and spend more when they do is an added bonus for the brand.

For West Elm, its success is not
so much the products it sells,
but how it sells them

For West Elm, its success is not so much the products it sells, though its products are cool and affordably priced, but how it sells them. Stores are not laid out to any corporate cookie-cutter design, but are individually crafted and made to feel and function as community hubs. The sales people are encouraged to think of themselves as 'merchants' and help customers not only with their home furnishings needs, but also direct them to other community resources, such as libraries, flower shops, theatres, whatever the customer might desire at the moment.

The concept: if West Elm makes a personal connection with its customers above and beyond their home furnishings needs, they will return to the store when they have new home furnishings needs to fill. It's a strategy that is working today, but perfectly poised for tomorrow.

West Elm is tapping the emerging demographic of young HENRYs that have a growing need for just the type of home furnishings that West Elm sells. Not only that, but the brand knows how to connect with – really connect, not just market to – this customer.

For brands that want to be successful with the young HENRYs, it is all about giving them new and compelling reasons why their brands and shopping experiences are meaningful and important to this digitally-empowered generation.

Marketing Starts with Understanding the Consumer

As a girl I discovered Nancy Drew, the young reader's detective series by mystery writer Carolyn Keene. I was hooked on the mystery genre. So I graduated to Sherlock Holmes and Agatha Christie, then onto other mystery writers, preferring the British authors like Dorothy Sayers, Ngaio Marsh, Josephine Tey, Ellis Peters, P.D. James and Elizabeth George, though she is an American, her mysteries are set in the U.K. and follow the traditions of the British greats.

My taste in movies and television followed a similar theme, preferring mysteries and police procedurals. I've often thought career-wise, I missed my true calling – to be a real-life detective. Yet as a market researcher, I'm just about the closest thing you can get to it, without having to deal with the blood, gore and guts of real detective work.

Mystery-novel enthusiasts and police procedural fans know that the detectives investigate the crime and identify the criminal by focusing on three perspectives:

- **Means** – Who had the means to commit the crime?

- **Opportunity** – Who had the opportunity to commit it?

- **Motive** – Most importantly, who had a reason to do it?

A market researchers' job is to understand the customers and the best potential customers. That takes detective work, which means we have to uncover who has the means, opportunity and motive to buy our goods and services. The same three perspectives apply to researching a new consumer market segment.

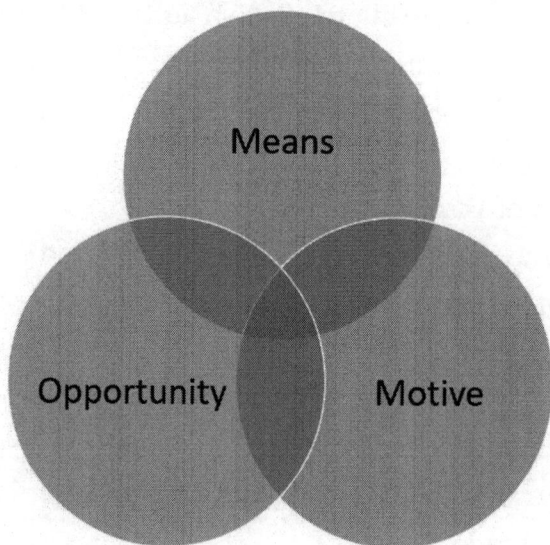

HENRYs Have the MEANS to Buy

The key to identifying the customer with means to buy home furnishings is understanding the demographics of HENRYs. Demographics give us the facts and figures that allow marketers to zero in on their best prospects. Income, gender and increasing age demographics identify the HENRYs, particularly the younger HENRYs, as home marketers' best new-customer prospects.

HENRYs are defined by income, $100,000–$249,900

The HENRYs term was originally coined by Shawn Tully in a *Fortune* magazine article in 2003 focused on the segment's heavy tax burden. But for home marketers, their spending potential is primary.

Affluent Market Segments by Income

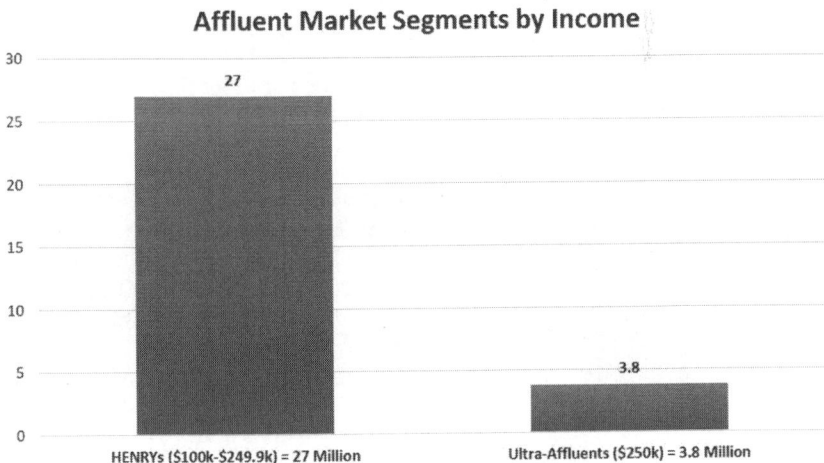

Bar chart. HENRYs ($100k-$249.9k) = 27 Million; Ultra-Affluents ($250k) = 3.8 Million

Unity Marketing defines the affluent as those with household incomes at the top 20 percent of the U.S. overall, which today starts just a shade above $100k. Among those in the top 20 percent, Unity Marketing's ongoing tracking study of affluent purchase behavior and spending has found two distinct segments in the affluent market: the Ultra-affluents, with incomes starting at $250k and representing the top 2 to 3 percent of all American households; and the HENRYs, the mass-affluent segment with incomes between $100,000 and $249,900.

HENRYs way outnumber the Ultra-affluents and while their individual spending power is far less than that found among Ultra-affluents, their overall impact on the U.S. consumer market is staggering. While the HENRYs make up less than 20 percent of all U.S. households, they account for about 40 percent of all consumer

HENRYs Contribution to U.S. Economy

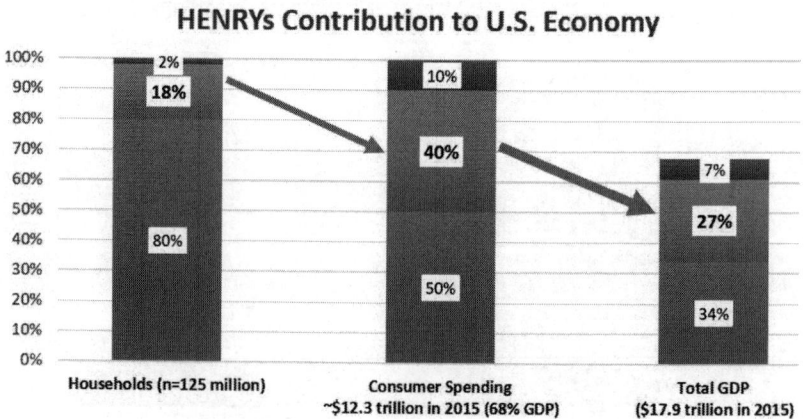

Source: Bureau of Economic Analysis, Bureau Labor Statistics, Unity Marketing
■ <$100k HHI   ■ HENRYs ($100k-$249.9k)   ■ Ultras ($250k+)

expenditures, which amounts to some $4.8 trillion in spending power.

As a consumer segment, HENRYs are the 'heavy lifters' in the consumer economy. They are doing better than nearly 80 percent of all U.S. households. And while the typical HENRY household doesn't have the spending potential of the Ultra-affluents, they remain an increasingly valuable customer segment for home marketers. That's because for every single Ultra-affluent household, there are seven HENRYs. Clearly, HENRYs are a market segment that home marketers in the high-end or aiming for the affluents' greater spending power can't afford to ignore.

Young HENRYs are more valuable to home marketers than Mature HENRYs

Affluence comes with middle-age, with income peaking from age 35-54 years, after which people start to retire, which tends to drive down the overall income of those from age 55-64 years. So for both HENRYs and Ultra-affluents the ages of 45-54 years specifically are when both segments' peak in terms of size and spending power.

However, HENRYs are far more heavily represented in the younger age ranges, 24-34 years than Ultra-affluents, as the younger HENRYs are growing in their careers with many of the most ambitious on the road to the Ultra levels of affluence.

Distribution of Households by Age

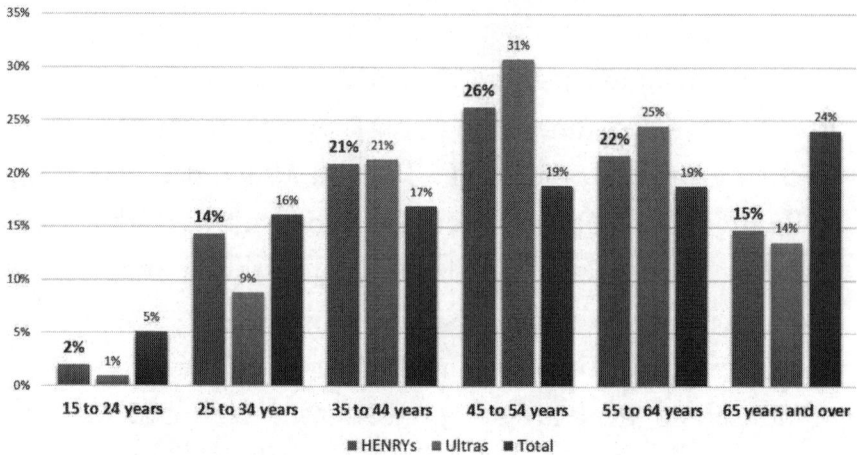

In Unity Marketing's affluent tracking study, in addition to the split in the affluent segments by income with $250k marking the line between mass affluence and ultra-affluence, two key age ranges, 24-44 years (young affluents) and 45-64 years (mature affluents), have emerged as significant to marketers aimed at the high-end and luxury segments.

Those in the young affluent segment are significantly more active in purchasing luxury goods and services, especially home furnishings, as they are in an acquisitive life stage where they are forming families, establishing households, buying homes and investing in luxuries to enhance their lifestyles. Mature affluents, 45 to 64 years, have already acquired many goods that define a luxury lifestyle and are transitioning out of an acquisitive mindset toward a more experiential one, often downsizing their homes as children leave the nest and their housing needs change.

This is not to say that mature affluents, including mature HENRYs, don't represent an important market segment for home marketers, but younger HENRYs, aged 24-44 years, are primed for buying things to decorate and enhance the quality of their lifestyles in the home. As a result, home brands as diverse as **IKEA, RH, Pottery Barn, Crate & Barrel, West Elm, Ethan Allen** and others have found success focusing on the luxury leanings of young HENRY affluents.

HENRYs' gender is less important than marital status

In certain marketing categories, gender plays a decisive role in the target market; however, in home-related purchases, especially among the affluents, marital status, rather than gender, is far more important. That's because the vast majority of affluents, both HENRYs and Ultra-affluents, are married and largely make home

Distribution of Households by Marital Status

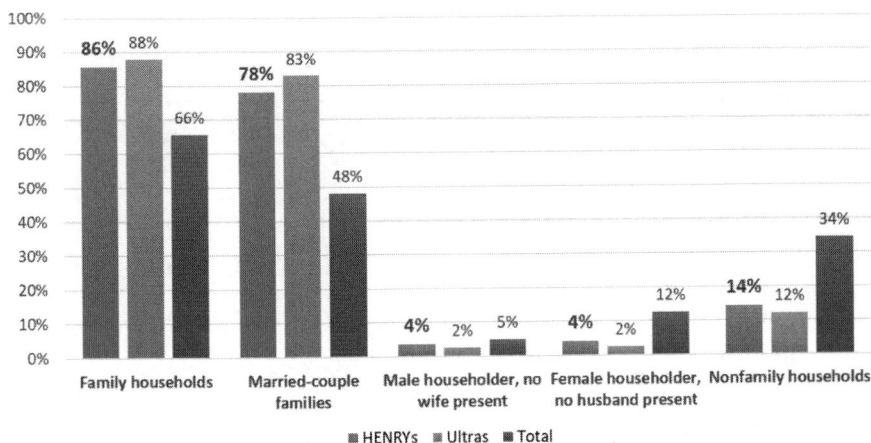

	Family households	Married-couple families	Male householder, no wife present	Female householder, no husband present	Nonfamily households
HENRYs	86%	78%	4%	4%	14%
Ultras	88%	83%	2%	2%	12%
Total	66%	48%	5%	12%	34%

■ HENRYs ■ Ultras ■ Total

decisions as a couple. Indeed marital status is a key demographic distinctive in the affluent market, since often it takes two incomes to propel a household into the top 20 percent.

As compared with the U.S. population as a whole where only two-thirds live in family households and one-third live in nonfamily households, over 80 percent of affluents, 78 percent of HENRYs and 83 percent of Ultra-affluents, live in a married-couple household. While HENRYs are slightly more highly represented in nonfamily households than Ultra-affluents, the differences are not statistically significant and can be understood by the higher representation of younger, still single affluents in the HENRY income segment.

Therefore, for home marketers aiming to capture the spending power of HENRYs, they need to be focused on the needs of young couples and growing families. That is the thinking behind **Ethan Allen**'s recent licensing partnership with **Disney** for a line of kid and youth furniture and furnishing.

High levels of education are another important demographic descriptor of HENRYs

A final characteristic defining the HENRY consumer is their high educational attainment. While only about one-third of all U.S. households are headed by a consumer with a college education, twice as many of the HENRYs, as well as Ultra-affluents (~66 percent) have attained a college degree or post-graduate education. This means that home marketers can approach the HENRYs and communicate with them at a higher, more conceptual, value-focused level than can marketers aiming at more middle-income consumers.

Final word of advice, given the HENRYs high levels of income, educational attainment and career focus, HENRYs often have budgetary responsibilities in their jobs. They are trained and have experience evaluating purchasing options and making budgetary decisions that maximize the return on investment in spending. They seek out and know how to identify the purchase options that represent the best value for their companies.

HENRYs don't leave their business smarts at the office, when they go home at night. Rather they apply the same due diligence in making personal purchase decisions. They know how to measure meaningful value in the home purchases they make. They seek out the best options that will deliver the values important to them at the most reasonable cost.

That calls on home marketers to communicate the value messaging around the brands and products they aim to sell to HENRYs. They aren't necessarily interested in the cheapest option, rather the most cost-effective one that delivers the value that is most meaningful and important to them.

OPPORTUNITY: Young HENRYs Are Primed for Home-Related Products and Services

Assessing your marketing opportunity with HENRYs requires understanding their shopping and purchase behavior. Past purchase behavior is typically a good predictor of future purchasing behavior, as consumers are more or less creatures of habit and so they tend to follow similar paths to purchase that worked successfully for them in the past.

The Bureau of Labor Statistics Consumer Expenditure survey, the nation's authority on consumer spending and the source used by policy makers in the federal government, identifies two key consumer segments where expenditures on household furnishings and equipment peaks: ages 35–44 years and household incomes over $100,000.

Admittedly, spending on home furnishings continues to be strong for those aged 45-64 years and rises as incomes rises over $100,000, but since almost all of tomorrow's Ultra-affluents start out as young HENRYs, these are the best customers for home marketers to make a connection with today that can lead to growth and prosperity tomorrow.

Connecting with the younger HENRYs is even more vital for home marketers' strategy because as they mature, HENRYs' housing needs are likely to change. From 25–34 years young people are in the household formation stage, starting their families and often buying their first homes. From 35-44 years they are likely to move up to their second homes and continue adding to their families. In the mature life stages, from 45–64 years, consumer also make predictable changes in their homes as they perhaps move up again, or invest in a second home. Then as children leave the nest and retirement approaches, they may move again to a smaller home, all the while continuing to have the need for new home furnishing and home decorating solutions.

Spending on Household Furnishings

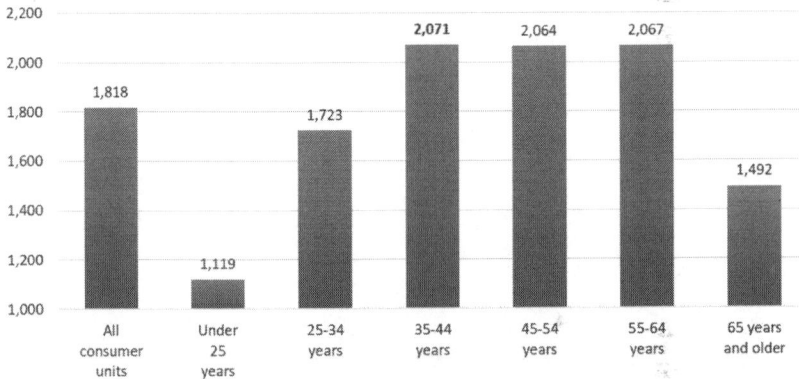

	All consumer units	Under 25 years	25-34 years	35-44 years	45-54 years	55-64 years	65 years and older
	1,818	1,119	1,723	2,071	2,064	2,067	1,492

Source: Bureau Labor Statistics, 2015 CEX & Unity Marketing

To dig even deeper into the young HENRYs' purchasing and shopping behavior syndicated market research studies, such as those published by Unity Marketing, can provide more insight. In UM studies we measure two independent but important variables that are key indicators of affluent purchase behavior in the home furnishings space:

- **Luxury home furnishings demand** – which indicates the percentage of affluents, both HENRYs and Ultra-affluents, that made a recent purchase of home luxury goods.

- **Luxury home furnishings spending** – the amount of money spent making those home goods purchases across 9 different categories, including furniture, floor coverings, outdoor luxuries, home electronics, decorative home accents and tabletop, linens and other soft goods, art and wall décor, major home appliances, kitchenware and housewares, and mattresses and sleep systems.

Included in those studies are the specific types of products bought in each category and where purchases were made. Here are highlights of recent Unity Marketing studies:

HENRYs have growing demand for home luxury furnishings

As far as demand goes, HENRYs are just about equally likely as Ultra-affluents to purchase any home goods during any of the three-month study periods. Statistically, there is no difference between the percentages of HENRYs and Ultra-affluents that make home goods purchases.

That being said, it is important to recognize that 65 percent of the 27 million HENRY affluent households that made a purchase of home luxury goods in 2016 amounts to far more purchasers than 65 percent of 3.8 million Ultra-affluents – 17.6 million HENRYs compared with 2.5 million Ultra-affluents.

DEMAND FOR ANY HOME LUXURY

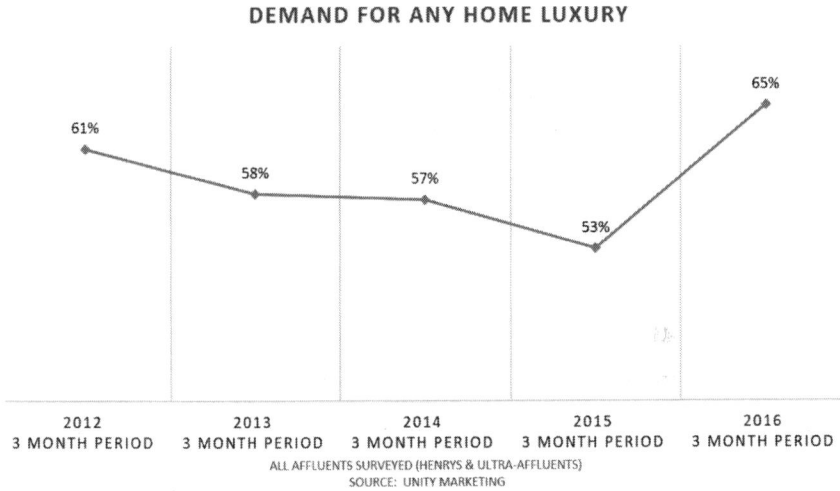

| 2012 | 2013 | 2014 | 2015 | 2016 |
| 3 MONTH PERIOD | 3 MONTH PERIOD | 3 MONTH PERIOD | 3 MONTH PERIOD | 3 MONTH PERIOD |

ALL AFFLUENTS SURVEYED (HENRYS & ULTRA-AFFLUENTS)
SOURCE: UNITY MARKETING

The home luxury market is deeper, wider and bigger among the lower-income HENRYs than the Ultra-affluents, who tend to be the primary targets of traditional home luxury brands. HENRYs represent a huge potential opportunity for home marketers.

But HENRYs aren't spending as much as they used to on home

However, while demand may be equal between the two affluent segments, the same cannot be said for spending. Ultra-affluents with their far greater income and wealth spend more on home luxury goods, though in the recent past the differences in spending between HENRYs and Ultra-affluents has been narrowing. UM data shows that Ultra-affluents are starting to spend more like HENRYs.

Affluent Household Spending on Home Luxury Goods

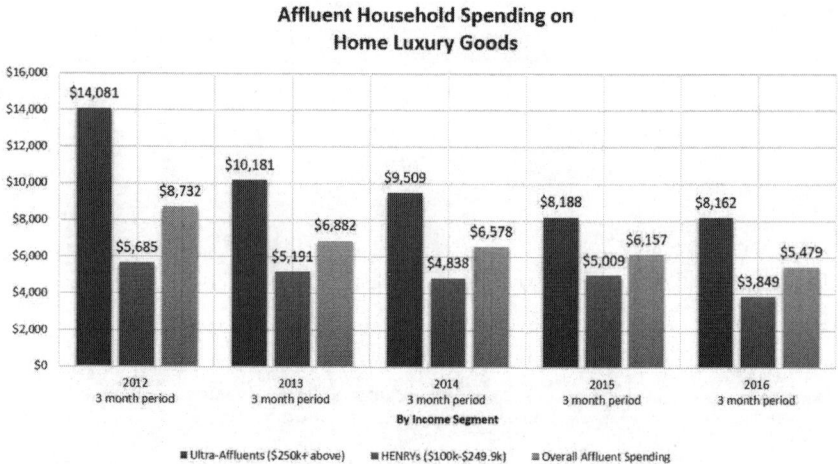

Ultra-Affluents ($250k+ above)   HENRYs ($100k-$249.9k)   Overall Affluent Spending

The survey reveals that spending on home luxuries has declined from 2012 to 2016 overall, dropping from $8,732 in 2012 to $5,479 in 2016 overall, with both HENRYs and Ultra-affluents cutting back their expenditures, even while demand for home luxuries increased over the same five-year period.

This pattern – demand on the rise, but spending on the decline – indicates that the affluents are spending less money on more purchases. Behavior shifts include buying at a discount, trading down to less high-end brands, selecting less expensive options (e.g., choosing accent pieces and fewer major furniture pieces), or economizing in other ways.

Where HENRYs shop for home furnishings is shifting

Disruption is a favorite word pundits use when talking about how consumers are shopping differently than they did in the past. While big national retailers, including **Macy's, JC Penney's** and **Sears**, are closing stores, other retailers, notably **RH**, are opening grander stores that offer new shopping experiences.

And then there is the internet. Amazon continues to expand its merchandise assortment to offer more and better things for the home and **Wayfair**, with its family of online brands, including **Joss & Main, AllModern, Dwell Studio** and **Birch Lane**, has grown from sales of a mere $601 million in 2012 to $2.25 billion in 2015, and net revenues for the first two quarters of 2016 are up 76.1 percent in 1Q16 and 60 percent in 2Q16 over previous year periods.

All in all, affluents today have a much wider range of home products to buy and places to buy them than they did a mere two years ago, not to mention five or ten. Unity Marketing's Affluent Consumer Tracking Study (ACTS) tracks where HENRYs, as well as Ultra-affluents, make their purchases in nine different home product categories. It reveals these as the fastest-growing channels for shoppers within each category:

- **Art & Antiques** – While art galleries remain HENRYs go-to destination for their art purchases, specialty home furnishing stores, department stores, and discount stores, outlets and warehouse clubs are among the fastest growing destinations to purchase art and wall décor.

And while the internet ranks second as HENRYs' shopping destination for art and wall décor, it isn't growing as fast as home furnishings, department and discount stores. This may signal that internet shopping, at least for art and wall décor, is reaching its peak.

- **Home Electronics** – For this category of goods, specialty electronics stores remain the destination of choice, but more HENRYs are also sourcing their television sets, audio systems and other home electronics from online retailers. To date discounters, outlets and warehouse clubs haven't made significant strides in capturing the spending of affluents in this category.

- **Furniture, Lamps, Floor Coverings** – Specialty home furnishings stores are the destination of choice for HENRYs when shopping for these goods, though their use of the internet has more than doubled since 2013 and home improvement stores has increased by 77 percent. These shifts make internet and home improvement stores the second and third most important destination for these goods. Of note, use of interior designers as a source for these goods declined from 13 percent to only 5 percent of affluent shoppers.

- **Garden, Outdoor, Patio** – Garden centers and the big-box home improvement stores capture the bulk of HENRY shoppers in this category, but art galleries that offer more artistic, hand-crafted items for the garden and patio are a rapidly growing source for these goods. Also trending are specialty home furnishing stores and discounters, outlets and warehouse clubs as a source for HENRYs garden decorating needs.

- **Kitchenware, Cookware, Housewares** – HENRYs' top three most important shopping destinations in this category are specialty gourmet cooking stores, internet and department stores, in that order. Except for a growing use of the internet for these purchases, there hasn't been any other significant shift in shopping patterns.

- **Major Home Appliances, Bath Fixtures, Building Products** – An important category for many luxury appliance and fixture companies, the HENRYs have been moving toward home improvement stores and the internet for these purchases, as they are less likely to frequent specialty appliance dealers and interior designers/contractors for these purchases.

  This suggests to brands that strictly limit distribution to designers and appliance dealers that they may want to broaden distribution to less exclusive channels in order to connect with high-potential HENRYs.

- **Linens & Bedding** – Department stores are the primary shopping destination for HENRYs when looking for home linens and since 2013 department stores have grown even more as a primary destination. Also posting growth in this category is luxury-branded boutiques and discounters, outlets and warehouse clubs. Interestingly, the internet reached a peak in 2014 but dropped back to 2013 levels most recently.

- **Mattresses & Sleep Systems** – The internet is the big news in the change in where HENRYs are shopping for mattresses and sleep systems. Use of the internet for these purchases has doubled since 2013, to be the second most popular destination for these purchases.

  Internet growth came at the expense of lost patronage in mattress specialty and furniture stores, though mattress specialty stores remain the number one destination.

- **Tabletop, Dinnerware, Glassware, Flatware** – Unlike other home categories, there is no clear winner as number one shopping destination for HENRYs when it comes to tableware. They shop widely across a range of stores, notably department stores, internet, specialty gourmet and tabletop stores, and specialty home furnishings stores, with the latter two growing in importance from 2013.

This gives an overview of the shifts and changes in where HENRYs shop for their home purchases by category. But for each brand and each marketer, distribution strategies will differ. It makes sense to go after distribution in the fastest-growing channels, yet as is the case in art and linens and bedding, the internet may well be reaching its peak, so moving aggressively to online distribution in these categories may not be the optimum strategy.

A key for any home marketer aiming to capture the HENRYs' attention and spending is to:

1. **Not be too exclusive** – Exclusivity to HENRYs feels undemocratic and too elitist, qualities that turn off more HENRYs than they attract. Your brand doesn't need to be everywhere, but it needs to be accessible and affordable.

2. **Partner with retailers that understand what value means to HENRYs** – Above all, HENRYs are looking for value when it comes to purchases for their home. Not necessarily the cheapest offer, but the one that offers the best value for the money. That means, pricing is not about how low you can go, but how much value you can offer. Pricing for HENRYs, therefore, hinges upon the value for

the shopper, not the price tag. So the retailers home-furnishing marketers partner with must put the customer and their values first.

The key to success in retailing today is not about WHAT you sell, but HOW you sell it. Make sure your retailing partners believe the same thing and are willing to focus on customers and their individual needs, desires and values in the retailing experience.

Deep Dive with Warren Shoulberg on the Current and Future State of the Home Furnishings Market

The home furnishings market was hit, and hit hard, by the recession. Not until 2014 did the home furnishings market claw its way back to its pre-recession levels, reaching $181.8 billion as measured by consumer expenditures.

But while the size of the home furnishings market may have recovered, the way American's shop for home furnishings, the brands they buy and their lifestyles have transformed since 2007. Disruption may not be strong enough to describe the marketplace home marketers face today.

Home-hungry HENRYs have new ways of shopping and new brands, like **Wayfair.com, RH. West Elm** and **PIRCH**, that offer access to innovative design ideas faster, more conveniently and cost-effectively than ever before. These brands are skimming the cream off the best potential market for home – the affluent customers with money to spend today. They are on the cutting edge with designs and selling styles that fit the next generation customers, the Millennials.

American Personal Consumption Expenditures
Furniture and furnishings

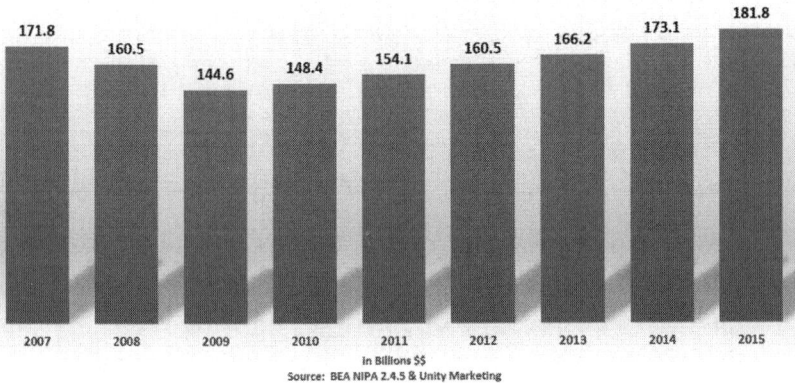

2007	2008	2009	2010	2011	2012	2013	2014	2015
171.8	160.5	144.6	148.4	154.1	160.5	166.2	173.1	181.8

In Billions $$
Source: BEA NIPA 2.4.5 & Unity Marketing

To help understand the challenges in today's and tomorrow's high-end home furnishings market, I sat down with Warren Shoulberg, editorial director for Progressive Business Media's *Home & Textiles Today* and *HFN* magazines and previously editor of *Home Furnishings News* for 10 years. Warren brings a long-term perspective to understanding the ways consumers relate to their homes, and the marketplace that has evolved to serve them.

Warren sees a bright future for marketers that can understand and tap the next generation of home owners – the Millennial generation, the leading edge of which turns 36 this year. While he recognizes marketers face

unique challenges capturing the potential of these consumers – "fewer households being started, an increasing number of renters with less need for some home
products, and demographics pointing to an emerging
less home-conscious consumer," he explains in his article for *The Robin Report* "Homeless in America" – he is
skeptical that Millennials will not be as home hungry
as their Boomer generation parents.

"A lot is being said about Millennials, like they don't
respond to brands or can't be coerced through marketing," Warren says. "But I am skeptical that they will
stay that way for their entire consuming lives. I hear
so many things said about Millennials that were also
said about Boomers when they were in their 20s and
30s, like we [Warren and I are Boomers] weren't going
to be conspicuous consumers. But we became the most
self-indulgent conspicuous consumers the world has
ever seen. I am not convinced that the Millennials won't
follow suit."

While marketers wait for Millennials incomes
and appetites for home goods to grow, opportunities
abound for brands that capture the attention and spending power of today's affluent home customers, as well
as the next generation's.

Home is where luxury lives

Luxury is a mindset, not a price point or a brand.
Millennials will still crave luxury for their homes, but

'luxury home' will be defined differently and more experientially. "What they are doing is defining high-end products differently from other generations. To them a luxury product may not be a **Louis Vuitton** bag, but a **Beats** by Dr. Dre headphone. So instead of buying the $9.99 **Sanyo** head phones, they are buying the $200 Beats one. That is how we are going to see their values expressed – premium products in different categories."

But we don't have to wait for these changes to occur, as today's affluent home consumers are already making tradeoffs in their home spending, as tracked by Unity Marketing's Affluent Consumer Tracking Study (ACTS).

High-end home brands need to tell a new story

Not only do Millennials want authentic brands (who knows more about how today's music should sound than music producer, rapper and entrepreneur Dr. Dre, aka Andre Romelle Young), but they want brands that connect with their values. High-end brands must explain what values are delivered along with their high-end price tag.

"In so many products, there is little perception of quality; soft home products particularly aren't differentiated," Warren says. "The consumers don't know what they are getting for the price. So if nobody is telling them why this $300 toaster is better than the $99 toaster, then they will buy the $99 toaster. They are willing to spend money, but the price has to be explained in a meaningful way."

This requires marketers to find new stories to inspire customers to buy their products. It's no longer enough to communicate just features and benefits, but to show how acquiring the brand will enhance the quality of the customers' lives, today and tomorrow.

Product overload results in customer complacency

People want what they can't have; that's human nature. But in today's consumer marketplace, home goods are ubiquitous. "Going to wholesale trade shows, you see 10 times as much product than ever ends up in a store. There is too much product, too few customers," Warren says.

With goods so readily available, aspiration to acquire good quality things is lost. He explains, "It's every-where, so if I don't do it now, I can do it later," is the consumer mindset. With the motivation to buy now missing, customers are encouraged, even rewarded, to put off purchases, since procrastinating customers can find lower prices if they wait for the inevitable sale that will come around.

Warren calls on home marketers to up their market-ing and branding game. They must differentiate their products and make the difference crystal clear through effective story telling. They must avoid cutting corners on quality and not be afraid to price their goods at a premium, but be sure to communicate the value. They must be authentic and trustworthy in order to give customers the confidence to invest.

MOTIVE – Why People Buy for Home

Understanding the motive to buy ultimately is the most important of all three perspectives. This is the psychographics or psychology of your customers and target customers. Unlike purchase behavior, which can change on a dime, consumers' underlying psychology is their set point; it characterizes their basic consumer motivations regardless of how other factors change.

A spend-thrift consumer tends to always be a spend thrift unless they make concerted efforts to change their behavior. A penny-pincher tends to remain a penny-pincher, regardless of whether they accumulate a lot of money or not. Just look at Warren Buffett, who is renowned for his thrifty personal lifestyle.

Motive explains why people buy, so that you can make sure through marketing efforts and shopping experiences that your offering meets their specific needs. So let's look more closely at the consumer psychology or psychographics of the HENRYs as it relates to their homes.

The HENRYs are a large, highly niched target market. You need to understand the different motivations that inspire these customers to buy so you can make a meaningful connection with your target customer.

As marketers we have to customize our marketing messages and the mediums through which we deliver those messages effectively so that they resonate, make an impression and inspire the consumer to buy.

Unity Marketing's research has identified five different personalities that make up the HENRY consumer segment. Think of the HENRY personalities like a pie cut into 3 fairly large and equal-sized slices of about 20 percent-25 percent, but with two slices shorted. That is the Temperate Pragmatists and X-Fluents.

Five HENRY Consumer Personalities

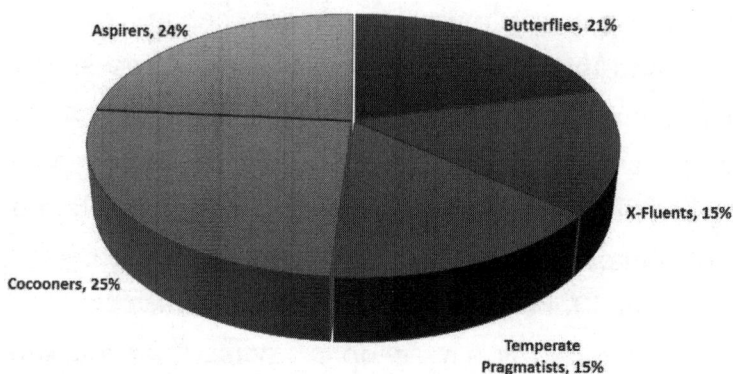

Aspirers, 24%

Butterflies, 21%

X-Fluents, 15%

Cocooners, 25%

Temperate
Pragmatists, 15%

For home marketers, three of the five HENRY personalities represent a strong potential market – X-Fluents, Aspirers and most especially Cocooners. The other two – Butterflies and Temperate Pragmatists – simply are not all that concerned with home (Butterflies), or less inclined to indulge in more higher-priced, premium products for their home (Temperate Pragmatists).

However, even the two least home-motivated consumer segments can be enticed, with the right positioning and the right marketing messages, to consider high-end home purchases as valuable to their quality of life.

Let's look more closely at each of the five HENRYs and how best to sell home goods and services to each:

X-Fluents live luxury 'large'

The X-Fluents are named for "extreme affluents," and among the HENRYs, only about 15 percent or so are classified here. That is because most HENRYs simply don't have the money to allow them to live luxury large as the X-Fluents do. For the X-Fluents, luxury touches every aspect of their lives, from the cars they drive, the way they decorate their homes, what clothes they wear, accessories they carry, and the places they stay. They are confident and live luxuriously for their own personal gratification, not to display their status to others. When marketers think about the quintessential "luxury consumer," they usually have the idea of the X-Fluents in mind.

But while X-Fluents enjoy luxury to the fullest, they may, or may not, choose the most exclusive and expensive brands. They are value-shoppers, not in the sense that they are looking for cheap or discount, but they are extremely focused on getting the most value for the money they invest.

So X-Fluent shoppers may love your $5,000 chair or your $10,000 leather sofa, and they certainly have the money to pay for it, but they might not be willing to buy it if the brand is too common, or another less expensive brand offers comparable quality and style. Today, the X-Fluents opt for value and a quieter, authentic and less conspicuous luxury lifestyle.

Aspirers want to be seen as players

The Aspirers, who make up slightly less than 25 percent of the HENRYs, have yet to reach the level of luxury to which they aspire. Aspirers are on their way up and want to be perceived as players. For them, luxury is about showing social status and prestige. They are less secure and confident than the X-Fluents, and believe that the glitz and the glamor that comes from the status-symbol brands they own identifies them as successful. However, their incomes may not yet match their aspirations.

So an Aspirer may want to own a showy $5,000 **Viking** stove or $10,000 **Lee Jofa** custom-fabricated sofa, but she may not be able to afford it. Aspirers are more likely to purchase the lowest-priced model of that brand's luxury range as a stopgap, or simply wait until their incomes catch up with their luxury aspirations.

This is the personality that brands that talk about the 'aspirational' customer are targeting. But fewer than one-fourth of HENRYs fit this personality and there are more male Aspirers than female ones. So those aspirationally-targeted messages are clearly missing the mark for the other personalities.

Cocooners express luxury in their homes

Cocooners account for another quarter of the HENRYs and are primed for home marketers selling premium-priced goods. Cocooners express luxury in and through their homes. Cocooners are all about the home; decorating it, furnishing it, surrounding themselves in a cocoon that makes them feel warm, secure, comfortable and happy. And they are core customers for well-designed, prestige brand bath and kitchen appliances and fixtures, high-end furniture and expensive home furnishings and decorative items.

Cocooners tend to focus their luxury indulgences on things for the home, not for him or herself. That means they may look more fashion victim than fashionista when out shopping. Their dressy won't signal affluence. As a result, a Cocooner might be overlooked as a good potential customer for more high-end appliances, furniture, decorative home furnishings and other items for the home. Cocooners also might be scared off if your brand or shopping experience is too X-Fluent or Aspirer focused and doesn't talk to his or her more traditional, hearth-and-home lifestyle.

But today many luxury brands, among them **Vera Wang, Ralph Lauren,** and **Fendi,** are extending their ranges into the Cocooners' home territory, so they are increasingly going to have to speak her language. They ignore this customer segment at their peril, because Cocooners are prime candidates for high-end and premium home brands. For Cocooners, the attraction isn't sophistication like for the X-Fluents or status like the Aspirers, but genuine quality and comfort in style.

Butterflies value experiences over things

Then there are the Butterflies who value experiences over material things. While HENRY Butterflies may enjoy a nice lifestyle and own many nice things, Butterflies prefer to spend their money on experiences, like travel and fine dining, rather than on material goods.

For Butterflies, luxury isn't what they own, but rather the things that they experience – and the joy they share with others from these experiences. When it comes to material things, quality premium or even mass brands, appeal to their sensibility as compared with heritage luxury brands, such as **Louis Vuitton, Gucci** or **Chanel**.

Butterflies can dress themselves and furnish their homes well with premium brands bought for less, while saving what's left to splurge on the high-end travel, dining and other experiences they crave. Home brands are largely missing out on selling to this highly experiential customer by focusing on selling the "thing," rather than focusing on the experience they have in shopping, buying, living with, and using that "thing."

The new **RH** (formerly Restoration Hardware) understands the Butterfly consumers and have found a ready audience of people not particularly set for acquiring more things for their home, but eager to participate in living the RH lifestyle, as well as enjoying the RH shopping experience.

Temperate Pragmatists are luxury marketers' worst nightmare

And finally there is the Temperate Pragmatist, who is a luxury brand's worst nightmare. Temperate Pragmatists view luxury with suspicion. For them luxury is just a marketers' label, not something that has any real meaning to them. They may enjoy a high income and personal wealth, but they would rather save it or spend it on things that are meaningful to them.

This personality is utilitarian and practical and oblivious to traditional marketing and branding approaches. Temperate Pragmatists are also concerned about the environment and the negative effects of the typical American throw-away, disposable consumer lifestyle. This personality recycles, repurposes, reuses, and makes do. Do-it-yourself very much appeals to this personality, as does the emerging 'Tiny House' movement popularized on **HGTV**.

They will steer away from overt marketing messages based on prestige, status and entitlement. They favor brands that are solid, well-crafted, long lasting and inconspicuous. A Temperate Pragmatist might own a **Viking** professional-quality stove or a **Miele** front load washer, not for the status, but for their engineering and durability. But they may decide that **IKEA** is just fine for their kitchen cabinets, and **Pottery Barn** for their living room sofa. This is also the target customer for the emerging renting and sharing economy.

Many young HENRYs show a decided Temperate-Pragmatic approach to shopping and buying. Living a Temperate Pragmatist lifestyle is in keeping with the younger generation's concern over the environment, global warming and the negative impact of excessive materialism. If your brand offers a lifetime's worth of use and can be positioned as a good lifelong purchase, you might get their business with that practical sell strategy. But they will not buy more than they need and they have come to learn that they can get by with much less indeed.

Marketers' Job: Make It Personal, Relevant, and Customized

In marketing, perception is reality. Marketers create that reality in the minds and the hearts of the consumer. A one-size-fits-all strategy for marketing to HENRYs, the high-earners with disposable incomes but not yet rich, and maybe never destined to be rich, won't work in today's increasingly diverse and sophisticated consumer market with so many good products available everywhere and at every price point.

An aspirationally-targeted home brand may well turn off an X-fluent as being too showy or trying too hard. The Cocooner might be ignored because they don't look like, dress like or act like one's idea of an affluent consumer, yet they come to the store with plenty of money to spend on their homes.

The Butterfly will be drawn to brands that promise an enhanced experience in the home, but those home brands focused primarily on look, not feel or comfort, may miss the mark. And the Temperate Pragmatist isn't tempted by traditional marketing pitches, yet if they consider the investment a practical, useful and good long-term investment, they may well purchase on the spot.

To market to the HENRYs, the gatekeepers to the emerging home market as well as the new target for traditional mass-marketers, brands need to understand the distinctly different psychology of those customers who have discretion and can afford their goods. That understanding will lead marketers to strategies to attract and inspire the HENRYs in their own language to invest in your brands – for their own special, unique reasons.

How HENRYs Are Changing the Home Décor Market

In targeting the HENRYs and their home decorating needs, the essential question all marketers must ask is what do HENRYs want for their homes? Unity Marketing has identified three key trends shaping the future of the home furnishings market based upon shifting values in the mindset of the HENRYs, particularly the young HENRYs on the road to affluence.

Smaller Spaces – Bigger Living

We've already mentioned the 'tiny house' trend as fitting perfectly the Temperate Pragmatist consumer psychology. But it's also an emerging trend across the entire younger generation of consumers.

Today people are seriously evaluating their lifestyles, what they need, what they own and most importantly, what they really need to own. It's a mindset focused on doing more with less and many young HENRYs are adopting the 'tiny house' mindset, even if they haven't yet moved into tiny houses.

It's a focus on quality of life, not quantity of possessions. It means they are making strategic compromises based on value. Here are some ways they are expressing it:

- Spending only $50 for a dinnerware set of 8 place settings, but $500 for a **KitchenAid** stand mixer.

- Buying a boxed wine for $20, but serving it in $20 per **Riedel** stem wine glasses.

- Paying $.49 per square foot for laminate flooring and $300 for an area rug at **IKEA**, but choosing to spend $500 on a **Dyson** vacuum cleaner and $2,000 on **Natuzzi** leather sofa.

> *HENRYs focus on quality of life,*
> *not quantity of possessions*

Confusing? Not to HENRYs! What distinguishes the choices above – KitchenAid, Dyson, Natuzzi, Riedel – is strong branding around a powerful quality message. Without it, a product becomes a mere commodity.

Home marketers need to use branding and marketing to make the value proposition crystal clear, otherwise HENRYs will opt for the cheaper choice.

Function **and** Style

It's substance over style for HENRYs. When weighing purchase decisions, HENRYs favor options that give them the utmost in practical utility and function over a choice that primarily looks good but is lacking in quality and substance. And if a choice offers both function and style to the highest standards, HENRYs will pay the premium required. They favor choices that don't require compromises, but when they have to choose, they opt for maximizing the functional and practical utility over style alone.

That's why **IKEA** is moving aggressively to enhance the quality and function of its home décor offerings. Known for its 'look for less' furnishings, IKEA determined its furniture needed a serious makeover on the inside to improve quality, so that its furniture is more durable and delivers more comfort along with style.

It's a strategy custom made for HENRYs, which is the second most popular HENRY home furnishings' shopping destination after **Bed, Bath & Beyond** in Unity Marketing's most recent Affluent Consumer Tracking Study.

Lust for Luxury – But It's Luxury in a Brand New Style

Especially among the Gen X and Millennial generation affluents, the old style of luxury has taken on many negative connotations. For them, old luxury reeks of over indulgence, conspicuous consumption, elitism, extravagance, conspicuous consumption, status seeking and, most especially, reflects income inequality and the excesses of the 1 percent. Brands need to market luxury in a new style that reflects the next generations' new values.

Mistakenly, too many luxury brands call the HENRYs aspirational, which implies their aspirations align with an out-dated style of luxury. Aspirational the young HENRYs may well be, but not necessarily for the old luxury that the brands are selling.

Rather, HENRYs are aspirational for an authentic lifestyle and true happiness, which research shows comes by what they do and experience, not what they have or own. The shifts in consumer psychology call on luxury brands to tell new stories. These young HENRYs reject their parents' and grandparents' ideas of luxury in favor of concepts that are more practical, functional, inclusive, democratic, responsible, and, ultimately, more affordable.

> *Too many young people believe that*
> *"luxury" is just a marketer's label*
> *that signifies something is over-priced*

Surely, HENRYs want high quality, superb workmanship, and all the other quantifiable features that luxury home brands promise. But they also want to align their consumer behavior with their personal values.

Too many young people believe that "luxury" is just a marketer's label that signifies something is over-priced.

So calling a brand luxury doesn't necessarily make it so. In fact, if you have to call it luxury, it probably isn't. The title of "luxury brand" must be earned in the mind of the consumers. It can't be a label that a brand claims for itself. Therefore, use the L-word with extreme caution and learn how to communicate luxury in a brand new style.

New Customers Demands New Ways to Market

In the first of its kind survey of luxury industry insiders conducted by Unity Marketing in association with *Luxury Daily*, "how to find new customers" rose to the top as luxury goods and services marketers biggest challenge to growth. The answer for home furnishings marketers is here: It's the HENRYs – high-earners-not-rich-yet consumers – especially the young HENRYs, aged 24–44 years.

For HENRYs, particularly the young affluents who will become the next generation of luxury consumers, making money, getting promoted, or becoming a partner is all well and good, but the traditional accomplishments are not the only prize they are after. Rather, it's the accomplishment of achieving a personal goal and digging deep to succeed at something truly remarkable, like completing an Ironman triathlon or doctoral dissertation.

These smart, accomplished young people know that by choosing the right profession and working hard at it, just about anybody can make a lot of money, if that is what one aims for. But HENRYs measure their success in ways more personally meaningful than just financial success. That's why for many HENRYs luxury-brand watches have lost much of their status-symbol cachet, since owning one mainly communicates financial status, i.e. how much money one makes and spends. Rather, HENRYs are looking for brands that communicate something more meaningful than just their net worth.

> *Young HENRYs reject their parents'*
> *status symbols in favor of symbols*
> *that communicate to their peers to*
> *which 'tribe' they belong*

For young HENRY affluents, there is a distinct generational component to their chosen status symbols. They reject their parents' or grandparents' status symbols, in favor of symbols that communicate to their peers to which 'tribe' they belong.

So HENRYs' status symbols are less about traditional high-end luxury brands and more about brands that really express one's values and identity. Think a **Mini Cooper,** rather than a **Mercedes;** or a **Filson** messenger bag, rather than one by **Louis Vuitton;** or a **Shinola** Runwell watch, instead of a **Rolex.**

That said, the **TAG Heuer** watch brand, after an unsuccessful attempt by corporate parent **LVMH** to move the brand upmarket to compete in the luxury price range of $5,000–$10,000, has recently reversed course, and brought the core of the product line back to a more affordable $1,000–$5,000 price point with new positioning aimed at the spirit and mindset of the HENRYs.

Even at $2,000, a TAG Heuer watch is still quite luxurious, but the new branding tagline, "Don't Crack Under Pressure," and its alignment with youth-skewing sports brands like Red Bull where it was just named the official timekeeper for Red Bull TV broadcasts, as well as celebrity icons, like Super-Bowl champ Tom Brady, super-model Cara Delevingne, and tennis star Maria Sharapova, are intended to resonate with HENRYs.

Getting to the "Why" of the Brand is Where the Future of Marketing to HENRYs Starts

In a recent talk at the Hackers on the Runway conference in Paris organized by TheFamily, marketer-extraordinaire Seth Godin asked "Is Digital the End of Luxury Brands?" Rather, the question should be "Is the Digital Generation, i.e., young HENRYs, the End of Luxury Brands?"

The key challenge for home brands and the young HENRYs is not about how they connect – internet marketing tactics, which are a given – but how to create new and compelling reasons why their brands are meaningful and important to this digitally-empowered generation.

Getting to the "why" of the brand is where the future of marketing to HENRYs starts. New branding and marketing strategies are what's needed, not just creative programming or digital-marketing tricks. It is all about tailoring the brand message to the unique psychology of younger consumers on the road to affluence.

Today, luxury brands telling old luxury stories of exclusivity, status, indulgence and over-the-top extravagance repel more than they attract. New narratives are required that maintain the elevation of the brand above the masses, yet connect with the unique consumer psychology of the next-generation luxury customer, which is democratic, not elitist.

This doesn't necessarily mean that traditional luxury brands must forsake the qualities and values that made the heritage luxury brand great, but pruning and shaping the strategies and the messaging to keep the luxury brand vital and relevant may be required.

Today too many luxury brands focus on new marketing and messaging tactics when focusing on HENRYs, while ignoring the strategic shifts that need to be made. And that requires putting the customer front and center. Give the HENRYs the luxury they really want, need and desire, and forget about the luxury the brand always gave them and thinks that they still want.

New Brand Stories for HENRYs

Luxury, ultimately, isn't a product or a price point, but a mindset. The core values expressed by the brand must link with the customers' values and aspirations. It's these people, not the product, that make a "luxury brand." Here are some new luxury stories that resonate with the zeitgeist of today's young HENRYs:

Performance Luxury

Luxury can't just exist as a product concept anymore, it has to deliver an experience that is meaningful to young HENRYs. It has to perform. That's the wakeup call for **IKEA** to improve the performance of its furniture line.

But performance luxury goes beyond merely performing under pressure of everyday life. Performance can also be measured by adapting to the needs of the hectic HENRY lifestyle. For example, the tabletop industry bemoans the fact that today's brides are not registering for traditional china dinnerware, in favor of more practical dinnerware alternatives that don't require special handling or care. Surely some of the bride's choices are driven by style, but many more are concerned about the white-glove treatment fine china, crystal and silverware entails. That's why **Noritake** has stepped up to the plate by proclaiming many of its fine china patterns "are every bit as dishwasher safe as our casual dinnerware," though freezer and microwave safe china still eludes the company.

The ease of use and care is also behind the origin of the **Riedel** O series of stemless wine tumblers. Offering the same distinctive bowl shapes as its Vinum stemware series, the O series promises to create the same enhanced wine tasting experiences customized to the specific wine varietal. But the tumblers also deliver added performance qualities, specifically "a glass that is easy to use; it will fit in any dishwasher, minibar or kitchenette, and even in a picnic basket. Broken stems are no longer an issue." And an added value: Riedel O series tumblers are significantly less expensive than the comparable Vinum stemware versions.

Luxury appliance marketer, **Miele**, is going after the same performance factors but from another angle – kitchen cleanup. The Miele G6000 dishwasher, which it bills as the "world's most advanced dishwasher," promises it can clean anything with no rinsing, even delicate dishware, along with "fleet design" that makes the model a "perfect complement to your entire kitchen suite." And while it costs many times more than the mass-market brands, Miele also promises 20 years of use, which makes it a smart choice for lasting durability.

While performance attributes differ by the type of home products offered, every home marketer has specific functional features it can highlight to make the brand the best choice for an informed, discerning customer. The key is to position its luxury as performing for the customer over the long term. The luxury of performance means it will work better and deliver meaningful value to the customer in their lifestyle. Performance quality counts big time for HENRYs and positions the brand as the smart choice.

Luxury of a Dual Purpose or Multi-Functional Luxury

The luxury of multi-function is a variation on the performance theme with a twist – the ability to deliver luxe performance doing different things. It's the idea of offering one item that can do more, giving the customer added-value for their premium investment.

Multi-function furniture is an idea that most of us grew up with – the convertible sleeper sofa popularized by **Castro Convertibles** back in 1931. But the sleep experience offered left much to be desired, presenting an opportunity for **CordaRoy's** to reimagine the convertible sleeper concept in the form of a foam chair that makes out into a more comfortable bed to set on the floor. Priced under $500 with washable covers, CordaRoy's offers a low cost, practical, multi-functional solution.

Other traditional furniture brands, notably **La-Z-Boy** and **Clad Home,** have taken the same idea of a sofa that also sleeps, but upgrade their designs to promise superior sleep comfort in an attractive, well-designed sofa. The result is these enhanced sleeper sofas perform both sitting and sleeping functions well.

Another take on multi-function luxury is offered by **Frame My TV** and **Hidden Vision**. In today's home, television screens are ubiquitous and intrusive. These companies offer decorative solutions to hide those screens. Frame My TV delivers decorative frames with mirrors or artwork that rolls up for television viewing and Hidden Vision features easy-to-install wall mounts with the television behind and a decorative mirror on the front so that television viewing is made easy by flipping the mirror up and out.

The 'tiny house' movement and challenges of apartment living have sparked a surge of creativity in multi-functional furniture, from coffee tables that convert into desks by **MainStays,** or ottomans that become seats by **Cubista**.

French designer Aïssa Logerot, of **AC/AL STUDIO,** has created a distinctive and beautiful folding ironing board that does double duty as a full-length mirror, but the design hasn't yet been manufactured. The idea was featured on **GoDownsize.com**, a website and blog that presents a wide range of dual-function furniture solutions along with helpful advice for living small.

The opportunities are wide open today for marketers to present HENRYs creative solutions to small-scale living challenges with more luxurious multi-functional home furnishings.

Luxury of Comfort

At its core luxurious home furnishings mean the ultimate in comfort. In a recent study conducted by Unity Marketing among interior designers, participants said over and over again that their clients' purchase decisions center around comfort. "Comfort is KING," as one designer expressed. Touch and feel matters more today than ever before.

Norwegian-manufacturer **Ekornes** makes the ultimate luxury of comfort the selling point in its line of Stressless collection of reclining furniture. It started with chairs that offered easy gliding technology which evolved to automatic adjustment of the headrest and lumbar support, promising "the most comfortable swivel recliner." Today it has further enhanced its position as the comfort-furniture king with a full collection of coordinating sofas with the same comfort DNA.

Interestingly, one of the key selling points for carpets and rugs is their greater comfort, yet few brands actually play up the comfort factor. Rather they focus on the functional aspects of carpets, emphasizing durability as this description from **Mohawk** illustrates, "You can count on industry-leading style, top performance, superior sustainability, winning value and unmatched service." But this emphasis on performance only gives credence to marketers offering hard surface flooring solutions, such as wood, ceramic and stone, which are the flooring category's fastest-growing segments, according to data from Catalina Research.

One carpet brand, however, makes the luxury of 'super soft carpets' its calling card: the Belgium-based **Sensualité,** by Associated Weavers. The brand positioning is pure luxury, "Sensualité is the embodiment of tenderness and strength, so cuddly yet so powerful. Sensualité is made up of four collections of unique broadloom carpet, each in a wonderfully subtle range of colours. The ideal carpet for a bedroom, full of softness, comfort and luxury." And the sensual appeal of the brands is showcased in its 'naked' glory on its website, featuring artfully nude models and embracing couples luxuriating on Sensualité carpet.

The luxury of comfort is a powerful selling point for home brands, since a key value of luxury is sensual pleasure. The comfort messages need to be communicated in words and pictures through marketing, with Sensualité doing an excellent job in that regard. But interior designers in the recent UM study also shared the importance of getting their clients to touch and feel their offerings to get them to buy. Designers have found that the best way to compete against RH, for example, is to take their clients into the showroom for a test sit down. Most of their clients find RH furniture seriously lacking the comfort dimension, whereas their more exclusive to-the-trade furniture brands, like **Kravet, Lee Jofa, Century** and **Hickory White,** deliver the luxurious comfort and quality that their clients are looking for.

Personalized Luxury

Personalized luxury is luxury that reflects the individual – who they are, their values, their identity, their unique personality. It's a rejection of traditional status symbols in favor of brands and icons that are highly personal and individualistic.

In personalizing luxury for HENRYs, brands remain important. Brands connect with customers by making them feel special. The brand presents a special, unique product experience that is relevant to its customers' lives and lifestyle. Relevancy makes the brand special and bespoke for the individual.

One brand that understands this need to connect through lifestyle expression of luxury is **Beekman 1802,** created by the 'Beekman Boys' Josh Purcell-Kilmer and Brent Ridge. Drawing inspiration from their New York State farm and back-to-nature lifestyle, Beekman 1802, which includes a store and online ecommerce website, offers a wide range of home furnishings that evoke the Boy's farm-to-table lifestyle with country charm but urban sophistication. As Josh says, "We try to approach the simple life with a little bit of sophistication."

The Beekman website features a high-end collection of tables, chairs, beds, dressers, accessories and more that "recapture and refresh vintage themes and techniques," as the website states, with many pieces using reclaimed barn wood and vintage industrial gears for an authentic patina. For those customers looking for a less premium expression, they've created a full line of home furnishings with **Target,** under the Beekman 1802 FarmHouse label.

In fashioning their brand, Josh and Brent reject the 'lifestyle' label, in favor of creating a 'living' brand, because the products they offer are "inspired by the life we are living," as Brent says. That is the authentic heart and soul of Beekman 1802 and their 'neighbors,' as they call their customers, are invited in to become part of their lives by engaging with the brand.

Rooms to Go offers another take on personalized decorating with its iSofa concept. Creating a living room design becomes as simple as answering three questions – Pick the style of sofa, select the color, and add pillows. Then with the assist of its website, the customer can add wall and floor type and color to see what their design will look like instantly in the home.

The design-conscious HENRYs also know that decorative accessories are the ultimate way to add personality to their homes. And they have no shortage of places to find those personalizing decorative touches. In fact, there are almost too many choices. That often makes a decorating decision overwhelming. So rather than luxuriating in their many choices, customers are confused and confounded, or as LA-based designer and author of *STYLED: Secrets for Arranging Rooms, from Tabletops to Bookshelves,* Emily Henderson describes them, "style paralyzed."

Thus the role of curator to help HENRYs discover and express their personal vision in their homes becomes of utmost importance. That curator may be a trusted retailer, like Mary Liz Curtin, co-owner with her husband of lifestyle and furniture store **Leon & Lulu** outside of Detroit in Clawson, MI or Mary Carol Garrity who operates **Nell Hill's** in Atchison, KS. Both retailers make artfully crafted merchandise displays in home-like settings a key to their success. It's a tactic that works in a retail setting, as Mary Carol emphasized, "People who shop here know that if they see it and want it, they better buy it. It won't be here the next time they come."

While some HENRYs think that professional interior design expertise is out of their reach, more are turning to the internet to find design professionals that offer customized decorating support online. Resources such as **Laurel & Wolf, Decorist** and **Havenly**, offer package prices to create a professional design that's right for HENRYs' budget.

Personalized luxury is more than just picking a fabric to cover a sofa or chair; it means helping customers create a room that expresses themselves and one that makes them truly feel at home. It is more than selecting a few lamps, a rug and some curtains. It requires service beyond just selling them 'stuff' and this service component is where the big opportunity for home marketers lies.

Create-Your-Own Luxury

Create-your-own luxury is all about self expression. It's the drive to become involved in the creative process, rather than just buying a 'thing.' It's a desire to get hands on in the creating of that thing, making it your own. It's this need that **Blue Apron** has exploited to such success selling meal kits that include all the ingredients and detailed instructions to create restaurant-quality meals at home. Since its founding in 2012, the company expects to reach half a billion dollars in sales in 2016 and has an estimated valuation of $2 billion, according to *Forbes* magazine. The idea of create-your-own luxury is tailor made for HENRYs.

For those handy with tools, **Lowe's** provides instruction guides and detailed materials pick lists to create-your-own woodworking projects, including tables, kitchen islands, and storage cabinets with desks, plus kits for other DIY furniture projects. And for those not yet confident enough to working with hammers, screws and nails, Lowe's has partnered with **Decorist** to offer custom-design services online.

While Boomers were once known as the 'Me-Generation,' young HENRYs have taken it to a whole new level. They are a generation raised on self-expression about everything, including their own skin, which has become a canvas for personal expression and creativity in the form of tattoos. The emotional drive for self-expression in home furnishings that adapt to all different room sizes and life stages is what **Lovesac**'s Sactionals furniture concept provides.

Lovesac is a brand better known for its iconic bean-bag chair. Today, Lovesac offers a uniquely customizable and innovative take on conventional upholstered furniture. Its Sactionals are described as a cross between "upholstery and Legos™." Sactionals consist of two basic upholstered pieces that can be combined in any configuration imaginable – no tools necessary – to create customized seating configurations from a compact loveseat for a studio apartment to a conversational arrangement to fill a super-sized great room.

With a starting price over $2,000 for a basic loveseat, Sactionals are quite pricey for many young couples starting out, but the add-on flexibility that allows the furniture to grow and change as the couple's needs change is the ultimate in luxury. Sactional furniture expresses an upscale performance vibe that delivers a personal experience in both design and function.

The consumer market in general is going more

experiential, valuing the things they do more than the material things they buy. Create-your-own luxury is a way to turn the thing you sell into an experience for the HENRY customer. There are many opportunities for marketers to engage their customers in the creative process so that they have more than money invested in their purchase.

That's one reason why **IKEA**, even while it moves to enhance quality in its home offerings, is never going to lose its ready-to-assemble concept. Yes, it is good for the company as it allows for ease of storing and shipping furniture in boxes, but it is also good for the customers because it makes them part of the creative process. They get special pride of ownership in creating and assembling their furniture.

Luxury of Craftsmanship

Many HENRYs today have a deep appreciation for hand-crafted, handmade items touched by a master. HENRYs look for the details that signal quality and care. It's a drive for authentic quality that the hand of a craftsman guarantees.

The luxury of craftsmanship is the story that has propelled the **Jonathan Adler** brand from the potter's studio into big business. Starting with his first collection of pots sold to **Barneys New York**, all of which he potted, packed and shipped personally, today Jonathan Adler Enterprises partners with home brands like

Kravet, Kohler, Formica and **Chandon** for home collections, as well as a new partnership with **Fisher-Price** for baby furniture, gear and apparel. JAE also operates 30 stand-alone stores, as well as sells products wholesale into 1,000 doors. Further, the Jonathan Adler website features a 'customize it' link that allows the customer to participate in the creative process to design textiles, casegoods and upholstered furniture in their own unique style.

Connecting craftsmen with appreciative consumers is the founding principle behind Brooklyn-based **Uncommon Goods**, founded by Dave Bolotsky in 1999 as a catalog which evolved into an online marketplace. Similar in concept to **Etsy**, the online crafters' marketplace, Uncommon Goods brings added value through curation, selecting the best designers from artisans and craftsmen all over the world. Products featured by Uncommon Goods tell the story of the artists and their inspiration.

Besides presenting authentic hand-crafted items, responsibility is also core value of the Uncommon Goods brand. It ships all orders in environmentally-friendlier packaging materials and favors artists who work with sustainable, organic or recycled material.

Ten Thousand Villages, a non-profit organization with 390 retail outlets, also makes doing good by supporting craftsmen and artisans from third-world countries the core of its luxury offering. It searches the world to find unique handcrafted products with every product telling its story. The mission is fair trade that creates opportunities for artisans in developing countries to earn income by bringing their products and stories to market. Ten Thousand Villages stores are located in many of the nation's 'high streets' that attract a more affluent customer.

The luxury of craftsmanship links the HENRY customer with the creative spark of the artisan. Through it, they participate personally in the creative process. It's a powerful way for marketers to tell a new story of luxury that resonates with HENRYs in an authentic and meaningful way.

Value Luxury

And finally, if you don't give them reason to pay more, HENRYs will always opt to pay less . . . and they can! **Wayfair, One Kings Lane, Overstock, Home Goods, Cost Plus World Market, IKEA, Pottery Barn, Pier 1** and many, many others are ready, willing and able to offer high style, high quality home furnishings for less.

More disruptive brands are getting in on the action, like **Parachute** which promises the same high-quality linens comparable to those from luxury brands like **Sferra** or **Matouk** at bargain-basement prices. Etailers like **Boll & Branch** and **Brooklinen** are capitalizing on the same idea: a more comfortable sleep experience for less. And paying so much less for the privilege, gives HENRYs even more reason to sleep well at night.

The lesson for home marketers is simple. Brands must deliver true value in line with HENRYs tastes and feelings. Selling on the cheap and discount offers are nice, but HENRYs are willing and able to pay up when the value is there. The key is to make the value message real and tangible, as Warren Buffet said, "Price is what you pay. Value is what you get."

Home marketers must use their marketing and branding to quantify the value story and make it real. When given a choice between the good, better, or best brand, they will go for the mid-point – better than good, but not quite up to the price level that best demands.

Marketers should aim for better or premium price on the scale: Mass market – Premium – Luxury high-end. Premium is that happy midpoint in pricing that will generate profits and growth for home brands. But the key is to tell the value story in real and meaningful terms.

Deep Dive into Power of Branding with Chris Ramey

In luxury circles, Chris Ramey is well known as an authority and thought leader on marketing, selling and serving the affluent. Formerly president of **International Design Guild**, the world's largest chain of decorative floor covering showrooms, Chris leads the **Affluent Insights** consultancy and **The Home Trust International**, a consortium of companies and designers that provide products and services for luxury homes. He's got his finger on the pulse of what is really going on in the high-end home and interior design industry, both from the supplier and the service side of the business.

Brand awareness is very low; there are few well-known design brands.

I recently talked with Chris about the challenges facing high-end, luxury home marketers, including interior designers that have primarily targeted the upper tier customers. When asked about the future of the interior design business, Chris says, "The challenges are profound. Brand awareness is very low; there are few well-known design brands. Then add the disruptive influence of the internet, **HGTV, Houzz** and other media that allow mass brands to pose as luxury. The result is a very different and unique path to purchase for consumers. And very little is good for traditional resources or professional interior designers who aren't, by and large, properly leveraging the internet or executing luxury strategies. And since so much of the noise is dumbing-down the industry, I don't think it's particularly good for consumers who possess the capacity for the best and deserve better."

Chris continues, "Amazingly, there remains a strange and misguided sense of entitlement among design professionals and design resources that they needn't do what the rest of luxury industry understands is necessary to find new clients and drive business – Branding!"

Part of the entitlement he refers to is the notion that the design trade has a lock on the luxury and affluent clientele. And as a result, they are losing share of wallet to other categories that clients care about. And they care because those brands and categories are investing in luxury marketing and branding strategies to create awareness and desire.

Case in point that Chris says illustrates this need is **RH** and its new sister brand **Waterworks**, both of which have strong appeal to affluent shoppers. "Interior designers increasingly shop at RH and Waterworks and therefore are less loyal to the to-the-trade brands that traditionally served them. It's proof that quality doesn't drive revenue; marketing drives revenue. These brands have done a very good job of tapping this upper-end market."

In other words, the consumers want RH or Waterworks brands because these brands have built awareness and desire. The result is clients may request these brands from their interior designers or simply side step designers all together and go direct to the source. The brand identities that RH and Waterworks have built in the mind of the consumers gives the customers confidence to make their own purchase decision, as well as gives them pride of ownership that they have made a good choice.

As Chris says, "The brands in the home say something about your sophistication as a home owner. A sophisticated and informed buyer acquires a **Steinway** piano, whereas a **Yamaha** piano provides different cues. A **Subzero** refrigerator says something about the home owner." Powerful luxury branding has established their presence of place in the affluents' homes. But too many home brands have not invested in such consumer-focused branding, and so have become increasingly commoditized as better marketed brands capture market share, in spite of the fact that they offer better quality, superior style, longer life and performance.

In marketing, customer perception is reality. The most successful brands are almost always the ones that invest most heavily in branding and marketing. If the customer thinks their new RH designed living room is state of the art in luxury and design, who can tell them differently? RH has already convinced them so.

The Need: Home marketers must talk directly to the clients through branding

"It is more important than ever to market directly to consumers," Chris calls out. "RH and Waterworks prove this point. Today's affluent consumer holds all the power. We have to create desire for brands and need to do that by communicating directly to the consumers."

He adds, "Any offering that is void of brand lacks value to the luxury consumers, since many customers don't understand the finer points of craftsmanship, quality and aesthetic that many traditional marketers emphasize. But they understand 'brand,'" as RH and Waterworks testifies.

The solution, therefore, is to bring brand forward in the industry and position the brand's values directly to the consumer. This advice is given to both the to-the-trade marketers and interior designers, who have traditionally relied upon word-of-mouth and recommendations as their chief marketing tool. But Chris says, "When someone tells me they get their business from word of mouth (WOM), that is code for 'I don't know how to market.'"

WOM may be favored, but designers need a solid foundation in branding and marketing to be truly successful. He continues, "For virtually every successful interior designer and every successful luxury brand or company, it is brand first, not product. Star architects and star interior designers are 'stars' because their marketing and PR preceded them. If you want to be very successful, you have to become marketers first." Need more proof, just look at Jonathan Adler.

The goal of that marketing is to expand the range of influence and communicate the value propositions directly to the people that most matter, and in this industry it is the affluent, including young HENRYs. "You have to think more strategically. You have to expand your prospect base with marketing if you want to grow."

Marketing Home in a Brand New Luxury Style

Marketing successfully to HENRYs takes new strategies. Here are some tips to maximize sales by attracting a more affluent HENRY audience to boost sales and generate growth:

1. Be Vigilant About Service

Nobody likes to go 'slumming' at retail, but some customers are more willing to forgo services in favor of cheap merchandise, or they simply haven't experienced better. HENRYs, on the other, may have tasted the high life at retail and know and appreciate high levels of service, including well-maintained merchandise, intelligent displays, and service personnel who know how to make the customers feel welcome.

It is this high level of service that is elevating **PIRCH** above the rest in the home appliance retail sector.

With eight flagship locations, including its largest that recently opened in Manhattan's SOHO district, PIRCH offers not only all the high-end appliances and fixtures one would expect, but also a broad range of selections that fit budgets for penny-pinching HENRYs, combined with unique shopping experiences that allows the customer to try out the merchandise before making a purchase.

Featuring only products for the kitchen and bath, and by not selling cabinetry or countertops, PIRCH maintains a laser focus on the functional, working appliances and fixtures that fill those spaces. The SOHO store has 30 different room-like settings, the company calls "vignettes," set up so that customers can test-drive the different appliances on the floor. For the bath, PIRCH stores also allow customers to reserve the "sanctuary room," where they can actually turn on the showerheads in the bath to select the right one for their homes.

With sales staff fully trained on the merchandise, along with onsite designers who can help customers plan their rooms, PIRCH is a fully immersive environment that brings customer service and the retail shopping experience to a whole new level. Robin Lewis, CEO of *The Robin Report* retail strategy newsletter, says PIRCH represents the future of retailing by creating an environment that is a "neurologically addictive experience." He stresses the experiences offered by PIRCH, rather than the things it sells, as Robin says, "Experiences period . . . are what it's going to take in the future for brick-and-mortar guys to survive."

Too many marketers make the mistake of thinking that retail is a product business, when in fact it is a people business. Today, customers can find good products virtually anywhere, and now, anytime, thanks to the internet. People go to the store to have an experience and to be treated well by other people; it's an incredibly important part of the package.

2. Showcase Quality and Workmanship by Telling Inspiring Brand Stories

Luxury marketers are experts about weaving stories around their brands to distinguish their high-priced goods from the ordinary, mass market offerings. To appeal to HENRYs, marketers must copy strategies from the luxe-branding playbook to set their products apart and above the mass. It can work for just about any product, even the lowly vegetable peeler.

The **OXO** company got its start when company founder, Sam Farber, observed his wife, stricken with arthritis in her hands, struggle to use a traditional vegetable peeler. This resulted in the design a new kind of peeler, easy to use, comfortable to hold and miles ahead of the competitive offerings in performance. The company today is owned by Helen of Troy, the centerpiece of its housewares segment, a $311 million business that grew 4.9 percent in 2016 following 7.9 percent growth in 2015. The brand includes over 1,000 home products of ergonomic-design and exceptional long-lasting quality that have won the company hundreds of awards.

With innovative design its strong suit, OXO follows a formal product-development process that starts with an in-depth exploratory stage where the consumer problem is studied and potential product solutions are identified specifying product features and target price points. Next the company sketches product ideas and material alternatives before creating models to test and play with. Next comes product design using 3-D modeling programs to see exactly how the product will work.

Larry Witt, the company's senior vice president of sales and market development, says it isn't uncommon for the designers to take a step back to the concepting stage for further refinement and customer needs analysis. Once a product goes through these processes, it move to the final phase where a tooling mold is developed and the first product samples are manufactured to see if in the hands of the customer, it actually does what is intended.

OXO succeeds by keeping the consumer and their using experience front and center throughout the design process. Marketing and branding then carry the ball forward to tell the story of the product, again from the consumer's vantage point. It is a formula for success for other home marketers too.

3. Innovate for HENRYs' Lifestyles

As HENRYs lifestyles change and their needs in the home evolve, marketers have new opportunities to innovate and bring forward new solutions to age-old as well as new problems. We've already examined the emerging opportunities to offer innovative decorative solutions for the small spaces that HENRYs are choosing to live in.

HENRYs' comfort with technology is also opening up opportunities for even smarter houses. From robotics, appliance tech, entertainment, and lighting controls to smart faucets and toilets, technology offers numerous opportunities for home marketers to offer innovative solutions to old problems. For example, inventor Doug Foreman, founder of Beanitos low-glycemic snack chips made from beans, identified a problem spreading cold butter right out of the refrigerator on bread and toast. Benchmarking the idea against atomizers that spray oil at the touch of a button, Doug came up with the Biem Butter Sprayer, a battery-powered appliance that instantly heats butter to the right temperature that allows the user to spray a shot of butter flavor and goodness, while carefully controlling the application and calories of butter indulgence without chemical propellants. It was an idea that got him a $500,000 cash infusion on *Shark Tank*.

But home innovation doesn't have to hinge on technology, either. Like the **The OneBowl** which allows you to cook pasta in the microwave, then instantly strain it and even eat or store it all in one bowl. Or **Bed in a Box** which allows the customer to order a memory foam mattress that is packed into a small box easy to ship and set up. The company also has a ready-to-assemble foundation offering the same ease of shipping and placement in the home.

There are many opportunities for home marketers to take an innovative approach to solve old problems in new ways, like **Lovesac** has done with create-your-own upholstered furniture. Or **Campaign** which recognized young HENRYs are on the move and needed furniture that was easy to transport and set up in all different types of settings. So the company designed break-apart upholstered furniture with a modern flare that ships in a box for on-the-spot assembly, but that also can be broken down and transported efficiently in pieces as young HENRYs move up and out of their starter apartments and homes.

The key is to identify the problem, research user needs, study various solutions with an eye to design, and test the concept with target customers. The big opportunity for home marketers is to transform the things you sell, and way you sell them, as **PIRCH** has done, into an experience.

4. Play to a Smart Shopper

HENRYs are above all smart shoppers looking for value but eager to maximize their return on their investment in spending. As mentioned, HENRYs don't go in for status-symbol buying, specifically spending more than they can afford (i.e., a **Rolex** watch) to make a social statement. In recent focus groups, a young HENRY lawyer shared that his status-symbol watch was his **Timex** Ironman Triathlon, which sends a message of who he is (an athlete) and what he values (practical, down to earth items), rather than extravagance and traditional luxury.

In HENRY circles, bragging rights come from getting a good deal, as well as being in the know about smart purchases. They do plenty of pre-purchase research online, evaluating their many options and finding the right combination of the values they want for the best price.

For example, while a **Viking** stove may be the brand that their guests will notice, the **GE** Café series of five-burner gas stoves offers virtually the same functionality for around $2,000 vs. $6,000 for the Viking. That makes the GE the preferred choice in an anti-status, smart shopper way – a new kind of conscientious consumption in a cultural environment that is demonizing income inequality and the excesses of the 1 percent.

5. Hit the Premium Pricing "Sweet Spot" Between Mass and Class

HENRYs, when given a choice between the good, better, or best of the best in any product or service category, pick the middle ground. They want something above the standard issue, but not something super exclusive and high priced. The best value by far can be found in the premium level, above the mass-market price, but below the luxury level.

Chicago-based **Interior Define** has specked out this premium space, offering many of the same furniture styling options previously only available at the custom, luxury level but priced right for discerning HENRYs.

Using a similar model described as 'radical transparency' as **Everlane** does for clothing, Interior Define lays out the pricing structure of its upholstered furniture against the typical model followed in the retail furniture business. In the name of 'radical transparency' it also explains the high levels of quality fabrication, structure and customization offered for all of its styles, giving the informed HENRY shopper the kind of in-depth information they can use to make a smart choice.

For example, Interior Define recently collaborated with Maxwell Ryan of *Apartment Therapy* fame to design a collection of upholstered furniture that offers the same seating luxury of to-the-trade brands, along with the same customization features including fabric and style of legs as previously available to the highest end brands, yet priced under $2,000. It's a powerful combination of value and price that is sure to appeal to HENRYs.

Take the Next Steps to Market Home to HENRYs

Understanding the HENRYs is critically important and will become more so in the coming years for home marketers that target customers at ALL pricing levels: down market, up market and everywhere in between. Prepare to meet this under-served but highly-motivated consumer segment by thoroughly researching opportunities in the HENRY market segment.

For Home Marketers Today, Market Research Is No Luxury, but a Business Necessity

Home marketers face a tsunami of changes in the consumer market that no amount of experience or education has prepared them for. The customers are changing faster than ever; they are:

- Adopting new patterns of shopping (start with the internet),

- Choosing new brands (walked a trade show lately?),

- Making new consumer choices based upon new values (for example, millennials would rather buy a new iPhone than a piece of jewelry), or

- Opting for no purchase at all (maturing Baby Boomers have got enough stuff already, they don't need any more).

And while marketers are trying to figure out where their customers have gone and why, there's a whole new class of upstart businesses to confront – Disrupters. The disruptors may well be foregoing profits today with the plan to take yours, and everybody else's, tomorrow after they completely make over the traditional way of doing business.

Because of these dramatic changes in the market-place and businesses' need to adapt rapidly and effectively, market research is no longer a luxury, something to put off until cash flow is stronger. The right kind of market research can reveal what's happening with your customers and your target customers – what they are looking for in their homes today and what they will be looking for tomorrow.

It will show you the new processes by which customers are shopping and selecting purchases for their home, among the widening range of brands and shopping alternatives that give them the right combination of function, quality and price.

Good market research delves into the critical issues in the distribution channels for home goods, and the day-to-day challenges marketers' existing channel partners face. Channel studies can help marketers identify opportunities they may have missed, as well as help their current channel partners prosper.

The right kind of market research will uncover the competitive environment, who the competitors are, and how they are encroaching on the established market.

Market research, including a competitive analysis combined with customer and channel partner research, can help marketers discover white space in the market, holes that a brand can fill with the right strategy and tactics.

But market research isn't enough. It needs to be analyzed and interpreted in such a way as to be actionable. It will become the foundation for a new marketing and branding strategies that take the research-based findings and create a road map for future marketing success. Unity Marketing excels at both – market research and marketing strategies.

Here's how to take the next steps to market home to HENRY:

1. **Dig deeper into the HENRYs:** Unity Marketing offers a range of in-depth research reports and studies about HENRYs, at affordable off-the-shelf prices. These studies delve into the HENRY demographic, providing detailed information about who these consumers are, what is important to

them, and why they will be more important in the future, plus many more case studies of brands that treat HENRYs right.

2. **Develop a system to keep up-to-date:** Unity Marketing's *Affluent Consumer Tracking Service* includes twice-yearly research that examines an affluent population that averages 66 percent HENRY demographic. The ACTS study is semi-custom allowing sponsors to ask questions to probe specific behaviors and interests, as well as add their brands and key competitor brands to the survey.

3. **Conduct customize research with HENRYs:** Need to go into greater depth? Contact Unity Marketing to learn how we can help your company assess your opportunities and prepare to meet the HENRYs head-on. Unity Marketing offers both qualitative and quantitative research services, as well as competitive, channel partner and market analysis studies.

Visit www.unitymarketingonline.com – Unity Marketing's website – or call 717.336.1600 to learn more about how we can help you tap the marketing potential of the HENRYs through our research reports and consulting services.

Index

About the Author

Speaker, author, and market researcher **Pamela N. Danziger** is internationally recognized for her expertise on the world's most influential consumers: the American Affluent. Her new book, *Shops that POP! 7 Steps to Extraordinary Retail Success*, reveals the secrets to crafting a retail shopping experience that's irresistible to high-value shoppers. As founder of Unity Marketing in 1992, Pam leads with research to provide brands with actionable insights into the minds of their most profitable customers.

Pam is a member of the renowned Leaders in Luxury + Design panel recognized by The Home Trust International. She received the Global Luxury Award for top luxury industry achievers presented at the Global Luxury Forum in 2007. She was named to *Luxury Daily*'s Luxury Women to Watch in 2013. She is a member of

Jim Blasingame: The Small Business Advocate's Brain Trust and a contributing columnist to *The Robin Report*.

She is the author of six books including a recent mini-book, *What Do HENRY's Want?*, which explores the changing face of America's consumer marketplace. Pam is frequently called on to share new insights with audiences and business leaders all over the world.

Pam and the Unity Marketing team is in a constant pursuit of new insights and understandings of these high potential customers for its clients. Toward that end, Unity Marketing conducts a biannual in-depth attitude and purchase tracking study among ~1,200+ high-end affluent consumers.

Unity Marketing's Affluent Consumer Tracking Study (ACTS) is the only longitudinal survey of its kind which provides not just a historic but forward-looking, predictive view of the affluent consumers and their attitudes toward spending and wealth in its exclusive LCI (Luxury Consumption Index).

Pam brings a passion for data coupled with a need to understand what drives and motivates consumers to Unity Marketing's syndicated and custom research studies. She uses qualitative and quantitative market research to learn about brand preferences, shopping habits, and attitudes about luxury lifestyles, then turns these insights into actionable strategies for marketers to use to reach these high spending consumers.